AF575878

HAMMURABI

JOHN BANKSTON

Mitchell Lane
PUBLISHERS
2001 SW 31st Avenue
Hallandale, FL 33009
www.mitchellane.com

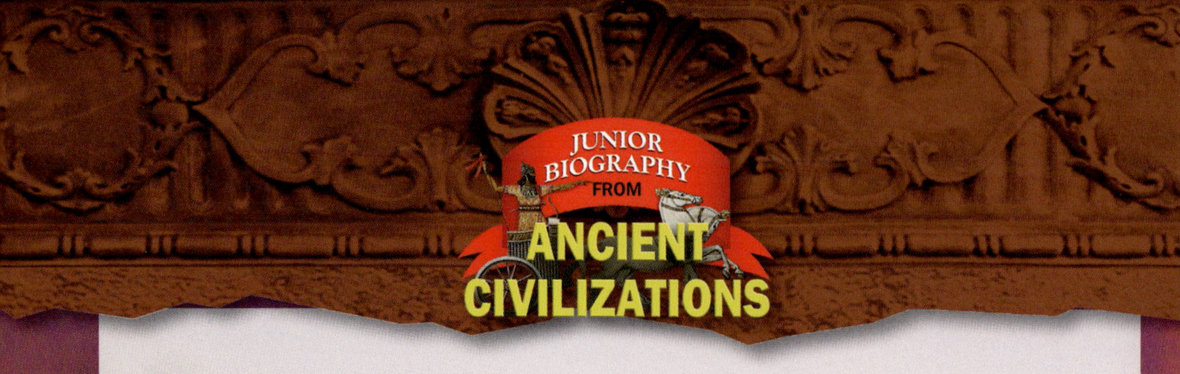

Alexander the Great • Archimedes • Augustus Caesar
Buddha • Charlemagne • Cleopatra • Confucius
Genghis Khan • Hammurabi • Hippocrates • Homer
Julius Caesar • King Arthur • Leif Erikson • Marco Polo
Moses • Nero • Plato • Pythagoras • Socrates

ABOUT THE AUTHOR: Born in Boston, Massachusetts, John Bankston began writing articles while still a teenager. Since then, over two hundred of his articles have been published in magazines and newspapers across the country, including travel articles in *The Tallahassee Democrat, The Orlando Sentinel,* and *The Tallahassean*. He is the author of over ninety books for young adults, including biographies of Alexander the Great, reporter Nellie Bly, scientist Stephen Hawking, author F. Scott Fitzgerald, and actor Jodi Foster. He is also a content writer for the business school website TopMBA.com.

PUBLISHER'S NOTE: The facts on which the story in this book is based have been thoroughly researched. Documentation of such research can be found on pages 44–45. While every possible effort has been made to ensure accuracy, the publisher will not assume liability for damages caused by inaccuracies in the data, and makes no warranty on the accuracy of the information contained herein.

To reflect current usage, we have chosen to use the secular era designations BCE ("before the common era") and CE ("of the common era") instead of the traditional designations BC ("before Christ") and AD (*anno Domini,* "in the year of the Lord").

Printing 1 2 3 4 5 6 7 8 9

Library of Congress Cataloging-in-Publication Data

Names: Bankston, John, 1974– author.
Title: Hammurabi / by John Bankston.
Description: Hallandale, FL : Mitchell Lane Publishers, 2018. | Series: Junior biography from ancient civilizations | Includes bibliographical references and index.
Identifiers: LCCN 2017009114 | ISBN 9781680200188 (library bound)
Subjects: LCSH: Hammurabi, King of Babylonia—Juvenile literature. | Babylonia—Kings and rulers—Biography--Juvenile literature. | Iraq—History—To 634—Juvenile literature.
Classification: LCC DS73.35 .B36 2018 | DDC 935/.02092 [B] —dc23
LC record available at https://lccn.loc.gov/2017009114

eBook ISBN: 978-1-618020-019-5

CONTENTS

Phonetic pronunciations of words in **bold** can be found on page 46.

This oil painting of Hammurabi is appropriately displayed in the Department of Justice building in Washington, D.C.

CHAPTER 1 The Lawgiver

His son had disappeared without a trace and the man thought that he was dead. But eight years later, the man heard a rumor that his son was not dead. He was a slave for a wealthy landowner.

The father traveled to the area where his boy was enslaved. The landowner admitted that he had the boy. But he refused to return the boy to the father so he could go back home. The father was not rich like the landowner. He did not have any power. There was only one person who could help him: **Hammurabi***, the king of Babylon.

Most ancient kings spent their time fighting wars and trying to expand the territory of their kingdoms. King Hammurabi did fight wars and expanded his kingdom, but he also made time for his people. After hearing the father's sad story, Hammurabi ordered the landowner to return the boy to his father. Then he went further. He ordered the landowner to be arrested and tried. It did not matter that the landowner was rich. He had broken the law.

Laws and rules affect everyone. Your school probably doesn't let you chew gum in class. Your

*For pronunciations of words in **bold**, see page 46.

parents might make you do your homework before allowing you to watch TV. If you play soccer, there are certain things that you can't do during the game, such as touching the ball with your hands. These are all examples of rules.

Outside of your school, your home, and your sports, there are many other rules. Drivers are not allowed to go over 25 miles per hour on some streets. Shoppers cannot take something from a store without paying for it. Employers can't refuse to hire a person because of the color of that person's skin. These rules are called laws.

Although Hammurabi was a king who ruled thousands of years ago, even the rich and powerful were expected to obey the law in his kingdom. A clay tablet had the message, "I am Hammurabi, the king of justice."[1]

Hammurabi created a set of laws called the Code of Hammurabi. Today, many of them seem odd or unfamiliar. Yet some of the ways in which laws are enforced now are connected to Hammurabi.

In the United States, voters elect the men and women who create new laws. These laws are written down and they usually apply to everyone. It was not always like this. For thousands of years, people did not have written laws, because a system of writing had not yet been created.

Early people lived together in small groups. They ate whatever they could kill or find in their environment. This was called hunting and gathering, and it was how they survived. Men usually hunted. Women gathered berries, seeds, and wild plants. They made their own tools and clothing. This way of life was not easy, and early people often went hungry.[2]

These early people were called nomads. They could not stay in any one place for very long since they always had to hunt for new game and find new areas for gathering food that hadn't already been picked over. Until around 9000 BCE, nearly every person on earth lived this way. Then it changed.

No one knows exactly when or why people became farmers. Perhaps the nomads noticed that the seeds they had dropped were beginning to sprout. Eventually they planted those seeds. They also began raising animals instead of just hunting them. That meant they

Great civilizations were born in humble farms, like those pictured in this illustration of Mesopotamia where animals provided both food and labor.

would stay in once place. Their days of hunting and gathering were over.

Many of the first farms lay in what is called the Fertile Crescent. This crescent-shaped region in the Middle East stretches from alongside the Nile River in Egypt to the Tigris and Euphrates Rivers in modern-day Iraq. Surrounded by desert, those rivers enriched the soil while providing a steady supply of water.

Farms changed the way people lived. After a nomad woman had a baby, she avoided raising another child until the first baby could walk. Permanent homes made it easier to raise more children. On a farm, young children who today would be in kindergarten worked alongside their parents in the fields.[3]

As more people settled in the Fertile Crescent, they established villages. As a result, more food had to be produced to take care of the growing population. Protecting the new settlements' farms and pastures was a matter of life and death. So villagers built walls and formed armies.

Village life allowed people to do other things besides farming. Some of them worked with metal, making tools and weapons. Others traded with people outside the village, bringing in different types of goods. There were also priests and priestesses, artists and storytellers.

Around this time, crude writing that used pictures instead of words came into being. Today signs with pictures meaning "bathroom," "walk/don't walk," and "hospital" are understood by people who speak different languages.[4]

Villages became cities and the very first ones were in Mesopotamia, which means "the land between the rivers." Mesopotamia stretched hundreds of miles along the Tigris and the Euphrates Rivers. Located in present-day Jordan, Syria, and Iraq, it is bordered by Turkey to the northwest, the Persian Gulf to the southeast, and Iran to the east. It became known as the "cradle of civilization."

Starting about 4000 BCE, people known as the Sumerians developed cities along the southern edge of Mesopotamia. They built

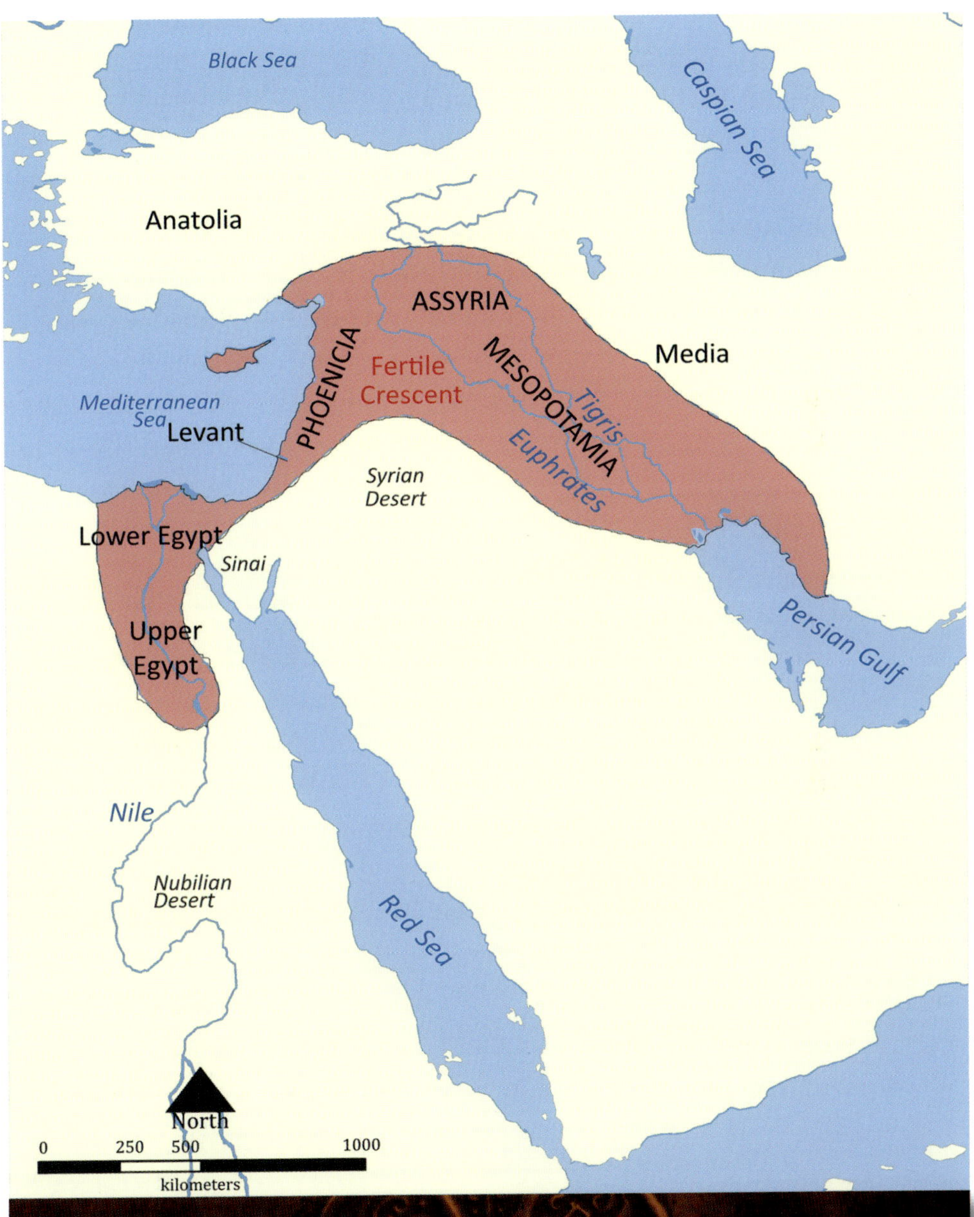

Today the Middle East is often viewed as a region of conflict, but over 10,000 years ago it was the site of the Fertile Crescent, where the first farms led to flourishing civilizations.

canals to carry water from the rivers to their farms. This is called irrigation. They constructed buildings like palaces and temples. These buildings required many workers, and the plans for the buildings required a system of writing.[5]

The first towns grew from tribes, which were led by a chief who made all the rules and also decided when to change those rules. As towns grew, so did the number of rules. By the time Hammurabi was born, the Middle East had many city-states. These city-states consisted of an urban center and the surrounding territory. They fought with one another for land and trade routes. Each one made its own rules. As Babylon's king, Hammurabi changed how his people lived, and his code of law changed how people thought about laws and justice.[6]

Mesopotamia lay between the Tigris and Euphrates Rivers. The place names in italics and three dots are the sites of ancient city-states.

Early Writing

The first writing was created around 3100 BCE. People wrote on clay tablets so they could record sales. The tablets had pictures of what was being sold, like grain or sheep. A wedge-shaped stylus was pressed into the soft clay to make those impressions. This was called cuneiform.

Since royal letters and accounts of wars and trade all had to be written down, knowing how to write was the path to a good job. Writers were called scribes. Training to be a scribe meant being in school for years.

Scribes wrote the history of Hammurabi onto clay tablets, and then Hammurabi approved what was written on them. After the fall of Babylon, those accounts lay buried beneath the desert for many centuries. Beginning in the 1800s, archaeologists unearthed many of those tablets. The words etched on them offer a window into the world of Hammurabi.[7]

The first writing was simple and crude but conveyed important information, like that seen in this Mesopotamian clay tablet.

Although this bust displayed in the Louvre Museum in Paris, France is called "the Head of Hammurabi," today it is believed to be far older than the ancient king.

CHAPTER 2
Birth of Babylon

Babylon, located about 60 miles southwest of modern-day Baghdad, Iraq, was perhaps the most famous city in ancient Mesopotamia. People began settling on the site about 2300 BCE. The city was sliced into two sections by the Euphrates River. The eastern part of the city was home to the king's palace and temples with altars to many gods. To the west, the residential quarter was built. Most homes were made of sun- or oven-baked mud bricks. These homes were built around open-air courtyards.

Almost nothing is known of Babylon's first centuries of existence. It enters the historical record at some point during the 1900s BCE. A ruler named **Sumu-Abum** founded what is known today as the First Dynasty of Babylon. His three successors did little to expand their borders.

About 1812, Hammurabi's father **Sin-Muballit** became the fifth king in the dynasty and ruled for 20 years. He added the nearby city-states of Borsippa, Sippa, and Kish to the original settlement. Babylon now included the area where the Tigris and Euphrates Rivers are the closest together. Many scholars believe that Hammurabi succeeded his father in 1792. We know almost nothing about the course of his life before he became king.

The society in which he began his rule consisted of three classes. The one with the least power was the slaves. When Babylonian troops won battles, the losing soldiers often became slaves. Poor Babylonian families who could not pay what they owed to the government or to the rich might also be forced to become slaves.

Above the slaves were craftspeople, merchants, and laborers who worked in the fields or on the city's many building projects. The third, and highest class, consisted of landowners, priests, and Babylon's wealthiest citizens.

Just as we know very little about Hammurabi's early life, little is known about Babylon's poor and middle classes. The thousands of clay tablets written during Hammurabi's reign mostly reveal details about the lives of the royal families and other members of the highest class.

Rich men inherited their homes after their fathers died. By then, they were usually in their thirties or forties. Their wives were often teenagers. The married couple shared the house with the husband's widowed mother, along with his unmarried brothers and sisters. A man had one wife unless she was unable to have children, and then he might have two.

Archaeologists have learned that even the wealthiest Babylonians ate simple diets. Although the Babylonians raised sheep, goats, pigs, and cattle, they usually ate meat only on special occasions. Normally they lived on a plant-based diet that included breads and soups, dates, and figs. They enjoyed sweets made with wild honey. They drank beer, which was made from barley. The royal families drank wine.

Special doctors performed ceremonies to drive out the demons believed to make people sick. Sometimes they might give

These slaves are at work constructing a large building in ancient Babylon. Slavery was common during this era of history.

prescriptions made of plants, herbs, minerals, or animal products to their patients.

Hammurabi might have attended a tablet school like other children of the wealthy. Although tablet schools helped educate scribes in reading and writing, they also taught other subjects. Organized much like today's schools, tablet schools had a head teacher or principal who oversaw other teachers in subjects like math and science.

A cuneiform mathematical text from Hammurabi's time. Most mathematical texts come from a site at Tell Harmel in modern Iraq and are primarily school assignments used to instruct students. Many are tables for multiplication, division, finding cubic measurements, or calculating weights. The Babylonian number system used the number sixty as a base.

The Epic of Gilgamesh

Babylonian schools may have had their students read *The Epic of Gilgamesh*. King **Gilgamesh** was a real person who ruled over the Sumerian city of Uruk around 2700 BCE. He was famed for his talents in war and in building, including the construction of a six-mile-long wall around the city. Long after his death, he was the subject of many fantastic stories throughout Mesopotamia.

The stories about Gilgamesh were originally spoken out loud. Eventually they were written down on clay tablets and turned into long poems called epics. These epics depicted Gilgamesh as a cruel king. He was two-thirds god and one-third human and he did whatever he wanted. His subjects prayed for protection from him.

Possible representation of Enkidu as Master of Animals grasping a lion and snake, in an Assyrian palace relief

The gods sent a wild man named **Enkidu** to deal with Gilgamesh. But instead of fighting Gilgamesh, Enkidu became the king's best friend. The two of them had many adventures together until the gods killed Enkidu. Gilgamesh's heart was broken but his character was changed. He became less cruel and more thoughtful.

The tablets containing the story disappeared many centuries ago. In 1853, archaeologist Hormuzd Rassam uncovered the 12 clay tablets containing the story. In 2003, German archeologists believed that they had discovered Gilgamesh's tomb, but the war in Iraq ended their planned excavation.

Worship of numerous gods was a vital part of life in Mesopotamia. This 4,000-year-old statuette was dedicated to Amurru, the ancient god of mountains and of wandering peoples.

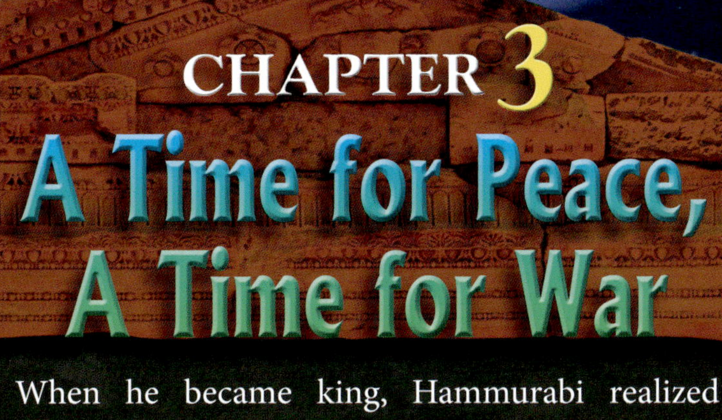

CHAPTER 3
A Time for Peace, A Time for War

When he became king, Hammurabi realized Babylon was not as large or as powerful as its neighbors. Some of the ancient world's most powerful kingdoms lay along its borders. To the southeast, King **Rim-Sin** controlled Larsa. Rim-Sin had defeated Hammurabi's father in a battle in 1810 BCE. To the north lay the Kingdom of Upper Mesopotamia. It was ruled by **Shamsi-Adad** and expanded 20 years before Hammurabi came to power. Weaker kings also hoped to expand, and Babylon faced threats from them as well.

In this situation, Babylon could disappear. To make sure his people were prepared to defend themselves, Hammurabi focused on gaining their support.

For years, many of Babylon's poorest people had taken out loans to pay their taxes. Those loans were expensive. As soon as he ascended to the throne, King Hammurabi forgave the loans, thereby making him quite popular. He gave poor Babylonians a clean slate and a new start on life.

Not everyone had debts, but nearly everyone worshipped. Religion was an important part of Babylonian life and the people honored different gods and goddesses. Each god had its own temple. Those temples were large and luxurious and had servants to take care of the gods' and goddesses' needs. Priests and priestesses dressed religious statues in fine clothing and jewels.

When Hammurabi became king, he donated part of the royal treasury to the temples and paid special attention to **Marduk**, the primary god of Babylon. Worshippers often prayed to him for help with any problems. Hammurabi said he "made great the name of Babylon, rejoiced the heart of Marduk."[1]

After five years of being king, Hammurabi's forgiveness of debts and temple improvements had strengthened his standing among his subjects. This was good since war was coming. Although the land west of the Tigris River was filled with productive farmland, the area near Babylon was becoming dryer. Today scientists believe temperatures at that time were increasing while there was less rainfall. This is called a drought. It was one reason Babylon and the kingdoms around it fought so hard for more land. They needed it for food.

Babylon was growing. Every year more children were born and more families moved there. Farmers needed land for crops and pastures for their animals. Merchants needed new trade routes so they could travel to other regions to buy and sell goods and products.

One important product was tin. Tin was important in Mesopotamia because it was combined with copper to make bronze tools and weapons. Bronze lasted longer and was stronger than tin or copper alone. The problem was that the closest tin mines were in Elam.

Elam lay east of Babylon, in the southwest corner of modern-day Iran. Already rich from controlling trade routes, Elam's wealth increased as it invaded its neighbors.

Marduk was one of the most significant gods during Hammurabi's reign. This image is displayed in the Louvre Museum in Paris, France.

CHAPTER 3

In 1767 BCE, Elam invaded Eshnunna, which was north of Babylon. Hammurabi was worried that Babylon was next. His army was not strong enough to defeat Elam. After Elam's soldiers attacked the Babylonian city of Upi, Hammurabi asked for help. King Rim-Sin of Larsa agreed to send soldiers to help defend it. They never showed up. "The army of Hammurabi that held Upi boarded ships and fled. Enemy troops have entered Upi,"[2] reported one observer.

Three years later Elam attacked Hiritum in Babylon. When soldiers leaned ramps against the city's walls to begin the attack, the townspeople were crafty—they opened their canals and the flood washed the attackers away.

But even as Elam's King **Siwe-palar-huppik** fought Babylon, he was weakened by his own army's unwillingness to fight. He begged Hammurabi for peace.

After defeating Elam, Hammurabi focused on King Rim-Sin, who had let him down. "Rim-Sin . . . has not changed his earlier attitude at all. He is hostile to Hammurabi. Military squadrons of his continuously enter into Hammurabi's country to pillage and steal. Every time they make an incursion, they take something back,"[3] a Babylonian official wrote.

In 1763 BCE, Hammurabi called upon his city's patron god Marduk to protect Babylon, and then he declared war on Larsa. The

This map shows the location of the kingdom of Elam and its location in relation to Babylon and other important ancient civilizations.

This ziggurat is part of a group of temples and palaces built in ancient Elam and known as Chogha Zanbil. The site was added to the World Heritage list of important places in 1979.

Babylonian army joined with two thousand soldiers from the city-state of Mari who were paid to join Hammurabi's forces. Upstream from the besieged city, Hammurabi's soldiers blocked the nearest river with bags of sand and diverted the closest canals. Those behind the city's walls slowly ran out of food. It took six months before Larsa surrendered. Now Babylon controlled all of southern Mesopotamia.

Then Hammurabi turned his ambition in the opposite direction. Mari, which lay northwest of Babylon, had helped him in several battles besides the one with Larsa. But Hammurabi attacked it anyway. In 1760 BCE, Hammurabi's army captured the city.

Hammurabi's army had protected Babylon's border and expanded its territory. After conquering Mari, the king ordered improvements on the canals and temples of the conquered areas. In fact, he was soon called *bani matim*, "builder of the land," because of all these projects.

Mari was briefly allied with Hammurabi and its troops helped him win several battles. Then he turned against Mari and destroyed it. Excavation of the ruins began in 1933.

Weapons of War

Hammurabi's infantrymen had several weapons when they met opposing forces in pitched battles: spears, slingshots, and ax-like tools with short curved blades mounted on one end called adzes. Trained archers used "composite bows." They were made of a combination of wood, horn, and animal sinews glued tightly together. They had a range two to three times longer than traditional wooden bows and more power.

But there was one weapon they didn't have. That was swords. At that time, weapons were made of bronze. A bronze sword would quickly lose its sharp edge and become too dull to be of value on a battlefield.

Soldiers covered their heads with conical leather or copper helmets. To protect their chests, some men wore thick leather, while others used bronze breastplates. Typically they would advance in straight lines, holding their shields next to one another to provide a wall against the flight of enemy arrows.

Hammurabi devised other types of strategy. One was constructing massive siege engines. Some would batter down the walls of cities they were trying to capture. Others were high enough to allow the soldiers to leap onto the tops of the defensive walls. Or his men might simply surround the city, cut off all access, and starve their opponents into submission. A third type was blocking the flow of the Euphrates and Tigris Rivers to downstream city-states. That cut off the water needed for irrigation and crop growth. Then the dams would be broken down, causing massive flooding.

Once buried beneath layers of desert sand, the prologue to the Code of Hammurabi was unearthed and is displayed in the Louvre along with the better known stele.

CHAPTER 4
The Code of Hammurabi

The expanding Babylonian empire was what today we might call multicultural. The conquered territories each had their own set of laws. A uniform set of laws, the Code of Hammurabi, helped unify the empire. Scholars believe that Hammurabi began formulating his Code in about 1772 BCE. As he conquered new lands, he decreed that his new subjects would be treated just like Babylonians. One of the Code's key elements was "to prevent the strong from oppressing the weak and to see that justice is done to widows and orphans."[1]

The Code was unique because the laws applied to everyone. Even the king was expected to obey the laws. For most of history, both before and after Hammurabi's reign, kings were seen as godlike. Kings could have someone murdered. They could steal and commit crimes for which their subjects could be executed. Hammurabi ordered his government to follow his laws. He said that kings must obey the law because it came from Shamash, the god of justice.

People often regard the Code as being especially harsh. Many crimes besides murder were punished by death.

The guiding principle behind the Code was what was later called *lex talionis*, or the law of equivalent retribution. That means the punishment is identical to the injury that has been caused. For example, the Code warns, "If a man put out the eye of another man, his eye shall be put out."[2] This is often referred to as "an eye for an eye." If a building collapsed and killed someone inside, the builder would be put to death. If a man killed another man's daughter, the father of the murdered daughter was allowed to kill the first man's daughter without being punished.

People's guilt or innocence was sometimes determined by what was later known as "trial by ordeal." In this type of trial, a man accused of committing a crime by another man would be thrown in the river. If he drowned, he was guilty and the accuser would be awarded the man's house. But if the accused man survived, that meant he was innocent of the crime. His accuser would be executed and the now-proven-innocent man would receive the accuser's house.

Hammurabi's Code covered many areas of Babylonian life. It made it unlawful to give an adopted child less of an inheritance after the parents' deaths than natural-born children. It gave women the right to divorce or to own property (something they would not have in Europe until modern times).

Under Hammurabi, Babylon was a free market economy. Merchants were allowed to buy and sell whatever they wanted and set their own prices. The code listed punishments and fines for dishonestly or poorly made goods and fraud.

While everyone was subject to the law, in some cases it might be applied differently. For example, a doctor could charge 10 shekels for treating a member of the upper class, five shekels for a tradesman, and two shekels for a slave. This cut both ways, though. If a doctor's treatments resulted in the death of a nobleman, his hands would be

A surgeon on trial in front of Hammurabi, accused of having caused the loss of the eye of a member of the upper class by an unskillful operation. If he was found guilty, his hands would be amputated.

The careful and almost identical looking cuneiform was probably nearly as indecipherable to most of King Hammurabi's subjects as it is to modern readers. In ancient Mesopotamia, only an elite few knew how to read and write.

chopped off. But if a slave was the victim, the doctor would only have to pay a sum of money to the master.

The Code also had an interesting take on robbery. A robber who was caught would be executed. If he wasn't caught, the victim would make an itemized inventory of his losses and submit it to his local government. Then the government would compensate him for the loss. If a robber killed someone in the course of committing the crime, the state would compensate the dead person's heirs.

Not only did Hammurabi's Code protect the free, it also protected slaves. There were punishments for those who killed a slave, and there were laws that stated how slaves could become free. "If any one fail to meet a claim for debt, and sell himself, his wife, his son, and daughter for money or give them away to forced labor, they shall work for three years in the house of the man who bought them, or the proprietor, and in the fourth year they shall be set free."[3]

A judge, however, determined most punishments. Hammurabi's Code governed judges and their judgments. It concluded with orders that the king obey the law

> in future time through all coming generations, let the king, who may be in the land, observe the words of righteousness which I have written on my monument; let him not alter the law of the land which I have given . . . if such a ruler have wisdom, and be able to keep his land in order, he shall observe the words which I have written in this inscription.[4]

Today, Hammurabi's ideal that laws should be equally applied is why his image is carved into marble in the U.S. Supreme Court.

Hammurabi at the U.S. Supreme Court

Between 1949 and 1951, the chamber of the U.S. House of Representatives in Washington, D.C. was remodeled. Twenty-three bas-reliefs of people who had helped establish the principles that govern American law were added. The image of Hammurabi is one, along with the ancient Hebrew leader Moses, the Athenian statesman Solon, and Thomas Jefferson, who wrote the first draft of the Declaration of Independence.

The United States Constitution established the Supreme Court. It oversees decisions made by lower courts, along with laws passed by Congress and executive orders signed by the president. The Supreme Court is therefore the center of justice in the U.S.

In the 1930s, Cass Gilbert, the architect for the Supreme Court, hired sculptor Adolph A. Weinman to design sculptures and friezes for the courtroom. Weinman designed two 40-foot-long, seven-foot-high friezes. One was affixed to the court's south wall, the other to the north wall. The overall theme was great lawgivers of history. It was up to Weinman to decide whom he would sculpt. He chose people like England's King John, who signed the Magna Carta, and Napoleon, the creator of a code of law bearing his name. Hammurabi appears between Menes, Egypt's first pharaoh, and Moses.

Today Hammurabi's contribution to justice is acknowledged in his depiction on a frieze inside the U.S. Supreme Court.

The Stele of King Hammurabi is topped by an image of the king receiving his laws from the god Shamash. The laws were inscribed on numerous steles like this one and distributed across Hammurabi's kingdom.

CHAPTER 5
Set Down in Stone

By 1750 BCE Babylon was perhaps the richest and largest city in the world. It was home to two hundred thousand people. It had a king so popular that boys and canals were named after him. Hammurabi had been king for more than 42 years and had accomplished so much. Now he did something to ensure that his fame and his laws would be legendary. He constructed a stele more than seven feet high that listed all the laws he had made.

On top of the stele is an image of Hammurabi as he receives the laws from Shamash, the Babylonian god of justice. Beneath it is a sort of prologue, which reads:

> When the lofty **Anu** [an early Mesopotamian sky god], King of the Annunaki and Bel, Lord of Heaven and Earth, he who determines the destiny of the land, committed the rule of all mankind to Marduk, when they pronounced the lofty name of Babylon, when they made it famous among the quarters of the world

> and in its midst established an everlasting kingdom whose foundations were firm as heaven and earth at that time Anu and Bel called me, Hammurabi, the exalted prince, the worshipper of the gods, to cause justice to prevail in the land, to destroy the wicked and the evil, to prevent the strong from oppressing the weak, to enlighten the land and to further the welfare of the people. Hammurabi, the governor named by Bel, am I, who brought about plenty and abundance.[1]

Then all the laws are inscribed, a total of 282. There may have been a few more but if so they broke off and disappeared in the centuries after it was carved.

The creation of the stele was one of the last acts of Hammurabi's reign. Scholars believe he died that year or early in 1749. His son **Samsuiluna** replaced him as king soon afterward.

Samsuiluna ruled for 37 years. He focused on holding onto what he'd been given. It wasn't easy. He was neither as strong nor as crafty a ruler as his father had been. At first he enjoyed the stability that his father had created, but then the kingdom began to deteriorate. Four more kings in the dynasty would follow him. The final one, **Samsu-Ditana**, was the ruler when the Hittites crushed Babylon in 1595.

More than eleven hundred years after Hammurabi's death, a new king restored Babylon's previous greatness on top of the earlier city's ruins. King **Nebuchadnezzar** II conquered Israel and he is mentioned in the Bible. This new kingdom is often associated with the famous Tower of Babel, though there is no way of proving this.

What is known is that Nebuchadnezzar's father **Nabopolassar** built the Great Ziggurat of Babylon and dedicated it to the god Marduk. It may have been as high as 300 feet (90 meters). Because it was made of sun-dried bricks, it slowly decayed. When Alexander the Great conquered Babylon—now under Persian control—in 331 BCE, he tore down what remained. He planned on rebuilding it but died before the project could be completed. Nothing remains of the structure.

Today, ruins of the Greek and Roman Empires stretch across Europe. In Northern Europe, evidence of the Roman occupation can be found in England and France. The Greeks proudly display ancient

According to the Book of Daniel in the Bible, King Nebuchadnezzar was insane for seven years. This 1805 illustration by English artist William Blake depicts the mad king crawling into a cave like a hunted animal.

monuments built to honor their gods. But the Babylon of Hammurabi was almost lost forever.

Modern-day Iraq is often viewed as a country divided by war. Yet thousands of years ago, its territory was one of the most successful places on earth. It is where the plow and the wheel were invented. It is where writing began. The world's oldest poems were penned in Mesopotamia.

But the kingdom Hammurabi ruled remains buried beneath the ruins of the rulers who followed. Only the words of the king remain.

Once home to one of the greatest civilizations in the ancient world, today Babylon exists only in scattered ruins, old histories, and Hammurabi's steles.

Home Away from Home

Had the stele with Hammurabi's Code remained in Babylon, it might have disappeared forever. Instead, in the twelfth century BCE, the stele was carried away as a trophy of war after Babylon was conquered by the Elamites. The conquerors brought it to the city of Susa, in the western portion of modern-day Iran, and put it on display.

About 500 years later, Assyrian invaders led by King **Assurbanipal** captured Susa and destroyed the city. The stele was buried in rubble.

In the winter of 1901, French archaeologists working at Susa dug up the stele. It was broken into three pieces. Iranian leaders had given France a monopoly on conducting archaeological research in their country. They also allowed the French to take whatever they discovered with them.

So the stele traveled to the famous Louvre Museum in Paris, where it was reassembled and restored to its former glory. Jean-Vincent Scheil, a Dominican priest who specialized in ancient history and languages, translated it. He is also credited with devising the way in which the 282 laws listed on the stele have been organized.

Code of Hammurabi from inside the Louvre Museum

Courtyard of the Louvre Museum and its pyramid

All dates BCE and may be approximate

1810 Hammurabi's father Sin-Muballit loses a battle to King Rim-Sin of Larsa; approximate date of Hammurabi's birth

1792 Hammurabi becomes the sixth ruler of the First Dynasty of Babylon.

1772 Hammurabi forms his law code.

1767 Elam invades Eshnunna.

1763 Hammurabi invades Larsa.

1765 Hammurabi allies with Mari and Eshnunna to attack Elam, which falls the following year.

1763 Hammurabi attacks Larsa with troops from Mari and other city-states; it falls six months later and Hammurabi now controls all of southern Mesopotamia.

1760 Hammurabi invades Mari and captures it; he orders improvements on canals, temples, and other structures in conquered areas.

1759 Mari rebels against Hammurabi, who puts down the uprising.

1755 Hammurabi controls all of Mesopotamia.

1750 Hammurabi has his law code carved on a stele; he dies.

All dates BCE and many are approximate

9000	People begin the transformation from hunter-gatherers to farmers, creating a stable food source and domesticating (taming) animals.
4000	City-states begin arising in Mesopotamia.
3100	The first writing is created in Mesopotamia.
2700	King Gilgamesh rules the Sumerian city of Ur.
2300	King Sargon of Akkad begins forming the world's first empire.
2150	*The Epic of Gilgamesh* first appears on clay tablets in Sumer.
2100	The city-state of Ur begins a brief period of superiority.
2000	Amorite nomads conquer Mesopotamia.
1894	Subu-abum founds the First Dynasty of Babylon.
1850	Amorites control Mari.
1822	Rim-Sin becomes king of Larsa and rules until 1763.
1749	Hammurabi's son Samsuiluna becomes King of Babylon; his reign is from 1749-1712.
1740	Samsuiluna loses control over southern Babylon.
1595	Hittite King Mursili sacks Babylon.
605	Nebuchadnezzar II begins reign in the revival of Babylon.

Chapter 1: The Lawgiver

1. Marc Van De Mieroop, *King Hammurabi of Babylon: A Biography* (Malden, MA: Blackwell Publishing, 2005), p. 127.
2. Jared M. Diamond, *Guns, Germs, and Steel: The Fates of Human Societies* (New York: W.W. Norton, 1998), p. 271.
3. Pamela D. Toler. *Mankind: The Story of All of Us* (Philadelphia: Running Press, 2012), p. 30.
4. Ibid., p. 37.
5. Diamond, p. 135.
6. Alexis Q. Castor, "Between the Rivers: The History of Ancient Mesopotamia." (Chantilly, VA: The Teaching Company, 2006), Lectures 20-22. DVD.
7. Toler, *Mankind*, p. 37.

Chapter 3: A Time for Peace, A Time for War

1. "The Code of Hammurabi," trans. L.W. King. Yale Law School: The Avalon Project, 2008. http://avalon.law.yale.edu/ancient/hamframe.asp
2. Marc Van De Mieroop, *King Hammurabi of Babylon: A Biography* (Malden, MA: Blackwell Publishing, 2005), p. 26.
3. Ibid., p. 34.

Chapter 4: The Code of Hammurabi

1. "Hammurabi," The History Channel. http://www.history.com/topics/ancient-history/hammurabi
2. "The Code of Hammurabi," trans. L.W. King. Yale Law School: The Avalon Project, 2008. http://avalon.law.yale.edu/ancient/hamframe.asp
3. Ibid.
4. Ibid.

Chapter 5: Set Down in Stone

1. Will Durant, *The Story of Civilization, Volume 1: Our Oriental Heritage* (New York: Simon & Schuster, 1963), p. 219.

Books

Barnes, Trevor. *Archaeology*. Boston: Kingfisher, 2004.

Chrisp, Peter. *Mesopotamia, Iraq in Ancient Times*. Brooklyn, NY: Enchanted Lion Books, 2004.

Gruber, Beth. *Ancient Iraq: Archaeology Unlocks the Secrets of Iraq's Past*. Washington, D.C.: National Geographic, 2007.

Meltzer, Milton. *Ten Kings and the Worlds They Ruled*. New York: Scholastic, 2002.

WORKS CONSULTED

———. *Mesopotamia: The Mighty Kings*. Alexandria, VA: Time-Life Books, 1995.

Castor, Alexis Q. "Lectures 20-22: Hammurabi of Babylon; Zimri-Lin of Mari: Laws," *Between the Rivers*. Chantilly, VA: Teaching Co., 2006. DVD.

"The Code of Hammurabi," trans. L.W. King. Yale Law School: The Avalon Project, 2008. http://avalon.law.yale.edu/ancient/hamframe.asp.

Diamond, Jared M. *Guns, Germs, and Steel: The Fates of Human Societies*. New York: W.W. Norton, 1998.

Durant, Will. *The Story of Civilization, Volume 1: Our Oriental Heritage*. New York: Simon & Schuster, 1963.

"The Epic of Gilgamesh," *Spark Notes*, 2014. http://www.sparknotes.com/lit/gilgamesh/context.html

Finn, Thomas M. *From Death to Rebirth: Ritual and Conversion in Antiquity*. New York: Paulist Press, 1997.

"First Monarch to Code a Nation's Laws," *The Mercury* (Hobart, Tasmania), October 8, 1937. http://trove.nla.gov.au/ndp/del/article/29221183

Foster, Benjamin R., and Karen Polinger Foster. *Civilizations of Ancient Iraq*. Princeton, NJ: Princeton University Press, 2009.

Matthews, Victor Harold, and Don C. Benjamin. *Old Testament Parallels: Laws and Stories from the Ancient Near East*. New York: Paulist Press, 1991.

Rufus Fears, J. "Lecture One: Hammurabi Issues a Code of Law (1750 BC)." *The World Was Never the Same*. Chantilly, VA: Teaching Co., 2010. DVD.

Toler, Pamela D. *Mankind: The Story of All of Us*. Philadelphia: Running Press, 2012.

Van De Mieroop, Marc. *A History of the Ancient Near East*. Malden, MA: Blackwell Publishing, 2007.

———. *King Hammurabi of Babylon: A Biography*. Malden, MA: Blackwell Publishing, 2005.

Waxman, Sharon. *Loot: The Battle over the Stolen Treasures of the Ancient World*. New York: Henry Holt, 2008.

ON THE INTERNET

D4K Dialogue For Kids—Archaeology http://idahoptv.org/dialogue4kids/season7/archaeology/facts.cfm

Ducksters—Ancient Mesopotamia, The Babylonian Empire http://www.ducksters.com/history/mesopotamia/babylonian_empire.php

"Hammurabi," The History Channel. http://www.history.com/topics/ancient-history/hammurabi

Mesopotamia Lessons, The Fertile Crescent. Browse the World, MrDowling.com http://www.mrdowling.com/603mesopotamia.html

The U.S. Supreme Court http://www.supremecourt.gov/about/briefoverview.aspx

The U.S. Supreme Court, Current Exhibitions http://www.supremecourt.gov/visiting/TempleOfJustice.aspx

The U.S. Supreme Court, North and South Walls http://ww.supremecourt.gov/about/northandsouthwalls.pdf

The U.S. Supreme Court Exterior Portrait Medallions and The Great Hall Metopes http://www.supremecourt.gov/about/medalionsandmetopes.pdf

Anu (ah-NOO)

Assurbanipal (ash-uhr-BAN-uh-pull)

Enkidu (en-KEE-doo)

Gilgamesh (GIL-guh-mesh)

Hammurabi (ha-moo-RAH-bee)

Marduk (MAHR-duke)

Nabopolassar (nab-loe-POE-luhs-sahr)

Nebuchadnezzar (neb-uh-kuhd-NEZ-ar)

Rim-Sin (RIM-sin)

Samsu-Ditana (SAHM-soo-dih-TAHN-uh)

Samsuiluna (sam-soo-ih-LOO-na)

Shamsi-Adad (SAM-see-ah-dad)

Sin-Muballit (sin-moo-baal-it)

Siwe-palar-huppik (SEE-wew-pa-LAR-hoo-pick)

Sumu-Abum (SOO-moo-uh-buhm)

PHOTO CREDITS: Cover, pp. 1, 4—Library of Congress; pp. 7, 9, 33—cc-by sa 3.0; p. 10—Goran tek-en/cc-by sa 3.0; p. 11—Photos.com/Thinkstock; p. 12—Rama/cc-by sa 3.0 France; p. 15—North Wind Picture Archives/Alamy Stock Photo; p. 16—Science History Images/Alamy Stock Photo; p. 17—Jastrow/public domain; pp. 18, 26, 39—Louvre Museum/public domain; p. 21—Rmashhadi/public domain; pp. 22–23—Pentocelo/cc-by sa 3.0; p. 23— Morningstar1814/cc by-sa 3.0; p. 24—peuplier/cc-by 2.0; p. 25—Pieter Brueghel the Elder/public domain; p. 29—Classic Image/Alamy Stock Photo; pp. 30–31—John Said/Thinkstock; p. 34—Mbzt/GFDL/cc by-sa 3.0; p. 37—William Blake/public domain; p. 38—U.S. Navy by Photographer's Mate 1st Class Arlo K. Abrahamson/public domain; p. 39—Benh/cc by-sa 3.0, SpirosK photography/cc by-sa 2.0.

GLOSSARY

archaeologist (ar-kee-AWL-oh-jist)—a scientist who studies past people and cultures by looking at objects from an earlier time

bas-reliefs (BAH-ree-leefs)—sculptures in which the subject is raised a few inches to give a three-dimensional effect

city-states—independent areas with a city at the center

continuously (kun-TIN-yoo-us-ly)—going on without stopping

cuneiform (kyoo-NEE-uh-form)—slim triangular elements used in the writing of ancient Babylonians

drought (DROWT)—an extended period of dry weather that injures crops

dynasty (DIE-nuss-tee)—a line of rulers from the same family

equivalent (ee-KWIV-uh-lent)—equal in value

executed (ek-si-KYOO-shun)—put a person to death as punishment for a crime

frieze (FREEZ)—a horizontal band decorated with sculpture

incursion (in-KUR-zhen)—invasion of a place

inheritance (in-HARE-uh-tens)—given money or things by a relative who has died

irrigation (ihr-uh-GAY-shun)—controlling water through a system of canals to help grow crops

legendary (LEJ-en-dair-ee)—stories told about an admirable person who lived in the past

nomads (NO-madz)—wanderers

patron (PAY-tren)—someone who supports a special cause

pillage (PIL-ij)—to take away money or goods by violence, usually in war

scribe (SCRYB)—someone who copies things in writing

stele (STEE-lee)—an engraved stone or pillar used as a monument

stylus (STIE-luss)—ancient writing instrument made of metal, bone, or other hard substance, with a sharp point at one end to scratch letters and blunt at the other end to rub out letters

ziggurat (ZIG-oo-rat)—a stepped pyramid-shaped temple in ancient Babylon with a shrine at the top